52 lessons for boys becoming men

Dedicated to my boys, boys everywhere and the parents who just want them to grow up to be good men.

Foreword

It's easy to be a jerk because you don't have to think about much to be one. You don't have to think about other people and their feelings. You don't have to think about your parents, siblings or friends. You don't have to think about your teammates or coaches or teachers. You only have to think about yourself and what you want at that moment. You don't have to think about the past or the future or the consequences of your actions.

To a jerk, there are no consequences.

But in the real world, there are, which is why — with a very few exceptions — jerks don't do very well in the real world. They may be talented, but they are lonely. They may win some games, but the wins don't last long. They may be funny for a little while, but eventually, people don't want them around.

Nobody wishes they had more jerks in their life.

I can be a jerk, and I remember the time in my life — the time you're living in, the time my own sons are living in — when being a jerk was really easy. I wish I had paid more attention back then to how me being a jerk affected other people. If I could go back to being your age, I would work really hard on not being a jerk.

You're learning a lot right now. Your life is changing. While I hate to be the guy who gives you more work to do, not being a jerk is too important to let it slide. That's why I wrote this book — for my boys, their friends and you. Take it slow. Don't try to read it all at once. There are 52 short lessons in this book because there are 52 weeks in the year. Take one of them a week. Read it on Sunday and think about it all week. Talk to your parents about it — or a coach, a friend, a teacher. Pay attention to what's going on around you. You'll notice other people being jerks, and I hope this little book gives you the perspective to judge for yourself what to do and what not to do.

Good luck. Let me know if I can help.

-CJH
May 2019

Don't Be a Jerk

Don't be a jerk.

There are a lot of people who are going to try and tell you things as you grow up. They will give you advice and tell you what you should and shouldn't do. Parents, teachers, relatives, coaches, mentors, friends, neighbors, grandparents — you're going to have a lot of information thrown at you over the next few years. Some of it will be great. Some of it will be confusing. Some of it will be helpful, and some will be flat out wrong. But if you have to boil it all down to a single piece of advice for growing up, it comes down to these four simple words: Don't be a jerk.

When given a choice between being nice or mean, be nice.

When someone needs help, help them.

When you succeed, do so gracefully.

When you fail, do that with grace as well.

Hold doors open and hold your tongue if you want to say something mean.

Be kind and brave.

Stand up for what's right and expect the people you care about to do the same thing.

Be nice to your parents and love your siblings — no matter what happens, they're the ones you've got.

Listen to people. Learn from people. Lead.

Be a team player, win or lose. When you win, remember the other team just lost, and you'll lose again soon.

Keep your head up, work hard and don't quit.

Care about your work, about people, about your things.

Be polite, but not a pushover.

Be tough when you need to be, but let things go when you can.

Move on.

No one likes a jerk, not even the jerk. Don't let your friends be jerks and don't accept other people being a jerk to you.

If you don't read anything else, just remember that everyone — every person on earth — has a part of them that is a jerk. There's a little jerk in all of us, and it will come out once in a while. But letting him out is a choice. You get to choose every day, even when no one is watching. Choose not to let him out as often as you possibly can. Even when a lot is going on. Even when the world seems unfair or scary or cruel. Even when it's easier to let him out than to keep him inside. Be brave and strong enough to do the right thing. In other words:

Don't be a jerk.

Swing for the Fences

There are two ways to be a batter: You can step up to the plate looking to hit, or you can go there hoping to not strike out. Be the guy who wants to hit.

Don't be the kid who hopes to get a walk. Don't let your team down by looking at the third strike. Don't swing at half speed. Don't be afraid to get beaned.

No one hits every time. Ted Williams, the greatest hitter to ever play baseball, is famous for hitting the ball four out of every 10 times he went to bat. But every single time he stepped up to the plate, he wanted to hit the ball. Every time the pitcher reached back and let it fly, Ted Williams was looking for a hit.

To be successful, you've got to swing the bat, and if you're going to swing the bat, swing it hard. Put some oomph into it. Go home tired after the game.

It's a good way to approach everything in life.

The author Hunter S. Thompson once said, "Anything worth doing is worth doing right." He was right. If you're stepping up to the plate, do it with a hit in your head. Focus on that hit. It will help with the fear. Let that hit be the thing that gets you back up to the plate every single time.

Be a hitter. Be an asset. Be the guy who wants to win and wins because he wants to.

Travel Light

Don't be the guy who can only eat eggs from left-handed chickens, or the guy who only sleeps on certain pillows, drinks a certain brand of artisanal bottled water or has to have every room at the exact same temperature.

Don't be the guy who makes other people work too hard just to please him or the guy who is so picky that he becomes a diva.

Unless there is a medical reason for certain preferences — food allergies, for example — learn to go with the flow. Even if there are medical issues, be prepared; don't make your needs become other people's burdens.

When I was leaving for college, my dad told me to learn to drink my coffee black. It wasn't because he hated cream or sugar, but because learning to drink my coffee black would mean that any time someone offered me a cup of coffee, I would be able to drink it. If I only drank coffee with a specific kind of cream or certain kind of sugar, and the person who offered it didn't have those things, I would be in the awkward position of turning their offer down. It might seem ungrateful or high maintenance.

Learn to be flexible. Learn to be easy. Learn to go with the flow.

Learn to travel light.

Honor the Line

The old woman had been waiting for her husband, who was at the other side of the counter looking at all the different kinds of pretzels available at the mall. They had been patient and waited their turn in the busy food court, but just as the cashier called for the next in line, a punk kid cut in front of them and ordered a frozen lemonade, which he paid for with his parents' credit card.

I cleared my throat and said, "Excuse me, but these people were waiting." This kid, who was maybe 13, shrugged his shoulders and said, "I already ordered, so, too late."

I have never wanted to punch someone in the face so badly in my entire life.

Situational awareness is more than just something your coaches yell at you about. It's about paying attention to what's happening around you, recognizing what's happening and acting appropriately. When you're driving, when you're in school, with friends, walking down the street, you always need to be aware of what's going on around you.

Had that kid looked around, he would have seen the older couple standing respectfully and waiting for their turn. He would have seen me, holding a baby, waiting behind them and, if he was a decent person at all, he would have asked if we were waiting and then taken his place at the end of the line.

The more time you spend staring down at your phone or a screen playing games, the less practice you are getting at being aware of the world around you. Wherever you go, look around. See if other people are waiting and let them go first. See if other people need help. See if there are other people you would be inconveniencing by cutting to the front and, if people are there, treat them like you'd treat your grandparents.

You probably won't get punched in the face.

Make Your Bed

Get up in the morning and make your bed. Your parents will be grateful. Your room will look better. Most importantly, you will feel better.

Making your bed is simple to do, and doing it proves you are responsible. But, more than that, it sets the tone for your day.

In a speech at the University of Texas in 2014, a Navy Admiral said the key to his success as a person and leader was making his bed every morning. You start the day by getting something done. It's something small, but it is an accomplishment. Getting something done early prepares your brain to get more things done throughout the day. If you leave your bed unmade, you've left something undone and kind of failed before you even got going.

As you get older, you will have more to do. Schoolwork, work work, practice, game tape, workouts. Your level of responsibility is directly proportional to your age. By the time you go to college or get a job, you won't have anyone following you around, reminding you of what you need to do. You'll be responsible for your own to-do list.

Making your bed might be small, and it might seem stupid — you're just going to unmake it again later to go to sleep, right? — but it's a great way to begin building your get-it-done machine. Think of it as a workout: You're developing your responsibility muscles. You get a little boost to begin your day as a bonus.

Get up, get it done, get dressed and get on with kicking the day's butt.

Control Your Hustle

Other kids will be bigger, stronger, faster than you. They will have good days when you don't. They will have bad days when you're on top of your game. There will be bad calls. You, your teammates, the coaches on either side will make mistakes.

In the end, the only thing you can control as an athlete — or as a student, son, friend, employee — is your hustle. You can't control other people. You can't control the outcome. You can only control how hard you work, how dedicated you are and what you are willing to do to accomplish your goals and contribute to your team and family.

Hustling means showing up prepared. Hustling means paying attention and doing your job. Hustling means putting in the effort to be the best you can be.

Jerry Rice had a gift for catching a football, but what set him apart from every other wide receiver was how he was the first player at practice and the last one to leave.

Other players were bigger and better, but no one was going to outwork him. Not just on the field either. He's famous for his dedication to his life after football.

Jerry Rice owns his hustle.

Hustle is not based on talent or size or intelligence. Hustle is a choice.

When you do your homework, do it as well as you possibly can.

When you do your chores, do them as well as you possibly can.

When you practice, don't let anyone practice harder than you.

When you play, be the hardest working player on the field.

The only thing you have control over is your hustle. Choose to make it the best part of your game.

Don't Blame the Ref

We've all been there. The game is on the line, the clock is running out, and just when you're about to pull a victory out of the air, the whistle blows, and you end up losing. A blown call blows the game. At that moment, you hate the ref. They stole the win from you. You want to explode.

The only thing is, it's not the ref's fault. Even when you think it is, it's not.

You are going to win. You are going to lose. The refs will make mistakes, and they won't. Either way, games never come down to a single call or a bad ref. Games are always the result of everything that went into them, every factor, every play, every player and coach. The ref is just one piece of a much bigger pie.

A lot of kids will pout and stomp. A lot of parents will lose their minds. They will whine and complain about the officiating. They will look like idiots and turn themselves inside out screaming.

Real players, real leaders don't look for people to blame when things don't go their way. They look for ways they can improve. They look to lift up and support their teammates. They look to the next game, the next practice, the next opportunity to get better.

No player in the history of sports has won every game they have ever played. The road to the hall of fame is paved with wins and losses, successes and failures, but it always moves forward. Don't get sidetracked by looking for other people to blame. It's poison and will only slow your development down.

Don't be the kind of person who takes all the credit for the good and blames the bad on others. Be the person who leads through the tough times and shares the credit. Be gracious and forward-focused no matter the outcome. Don't blame the ref.

Running Beats Talent

Talent will get you on the team, but hard work and concentration will win you the MVP award at the end of the season.

Talent is a great thing to have. Being good at something makes a lot of people want to get better. Getting better helps you stand out.

But there is a big difference between being talented and being valuable. There are talented kids who, when things are going their way, will win games. But a lot of talented people rely on their talent to cover for their lack of competitiveness, their laziness, their lack of winning attitude.

There was a very talented player on my high school tennis team. He was fast, strong, had great command. When he was on his game, he was unbeatable. But when the match was close, he gave up. He started blaming the wind or the balls, his racquet or the umpire for not giving him the close calls. At the end of our sophomore year, he had won almost 80% of his matches, which is very impressive. Winning that much usually makes you the clear favorite.

But at the year-end banquet, this incredibly talented tennis player did not get the MVP award. That honor went, instead, to a less talented player who only won about 60% of his matches.

Why?

Because when the talented player lost, he lost big. He gave up. He stopped trying and let the player on the other side of the net beat him.

When the MVP lost, his matches were closer. He never gave up, even when he was outmatched, and it was clear from the first volley that he was going to lose. He would be facing triple match point and he still fought for every shot, every serve, every volley.

When the talented player lost, he barely recognized the person he had been playing. Even though it's customary (in fact, required) to shake the other player's hand, he would do so with his head hung low, muttering to himself one excuse after another.

When the MVP lost, he jogged to the net, extended his hand and congratulated the person who beat him. He looked him in the eye and complimented one shot or another.

The last I heard, the talented player quit college tennis when he was unsuccessful. The MVP? He's one of the most successful tennis coaches in the state.

Talent is a good thing, but the ability to outwork everyone, support your teammates, listen to your coaches and learn from your losses will take you even further.

Be Nice to Your Mom

Okay, here's the deal: She may be on you to clean your room, do your homework or pick up your mess; she may be on you to stand up straight, eat your veggies and make your bed, but, I promise you, there is no one who loves you more or is more deserving of your effort, affection and love than your mom.

Moms work their butts off. They keep you healthy, manage your schedule, keep you clothed, fed and doing well in school. They think about your needs and the future. They think about your birthday and your graduation day. They make sure you get your time with friends and are enrolled in all your activities. They make your life what it is.

Plus, she made you. Literally, she made you. Let that sink in.

Someday, you will have a relationship with someone you want to impress. You'll fall in love and think about building a life together. One of the things your future partner will look for in you is how you treat your mom because how a man treats his mom is directly related to how he may treat his partner. If he is selfish, if he is self-centered and dismissive, these will be GIANT red flags.

But if he is considerate and respectful, if he shows love and devotion, it is a massive plus to his credit.

Be nice to your mom. Love her. Help her. Listen to her. Respect her. Thank her. She deserves it more than you can possibly know, and you will be better off for treating her right.

And eat your vegetables, for God's sake.

Learn to Make Eggs

Every man should be able to make breakfast, so you might as well learn how to do it now. It's not hard, and being able to cook eggs means you won't have to rely on your parents or pre-packaged crap food when you're hungry. When you get to college, it will make you popular. When you're out on your own, it will give you comfort. When you have a family, it will be a bonding experience with your kids.

A dozen eggs will cost you less than five dollars. A stick of butter is cheap. Salt and pepper are almost free. Here are three can't-miss recipes. Get a dozen eggs and practice until perfect.

Scrambled Eggs

Put a small skillet — the low, flat pan with the handle — over low heat, marked either "Low" or "2" on the stovetop.

Put 2 tablespoons of butter — unsalted — into the pan and let it melt. Swirl the melted butter around the pan to coat the bottom, but don't let it burn.

Crack two eggs into the pan once the butter is melted. Using a silicone or wooden spatula, stir vigorously until the yolks and whites are blended. The more and harder you stir, the fluffier the eggs will be.

Let it sit for a minute or so, and then begin stirring the mixture slowly around the pan. It should start coming together, becoming more solid. Keep it moving so it doesn't burn.

Do this until the eggs are solid and not shiny. Remove from heat. Add some salt and pepper, put the eggs on a plate and eat it.

Five minutes, and you've got breakfast.

Over-Medium Eggs

Spray a little cooking spray — or a little olive oil, or 2 tablespoons of butter — onto a small skillet on low to low-medium heat.

Once the pan is coated with the spray, oil or butter, crack two eggs into the pan. Try not to break the yolks.

Cover and let it cook for a minute or two, until the whites are cooked.

Once the whites are cooked, use a rubber, silicone or wooden spatula to carefully turn the eggs over. Don't rush this; be gentle to keep the yolks intact.

Let sit for 30 to 60 seconds, depending upon how cooked you like your yolks. (I like mine runny, so I only let it cook for 15-20 seconds.)

When the yolk is cooked how you like it, put the eggs on the plate, add some salt, pepper and hot sauce, and enjoy.

Bam, breakfast is served.

Hard-Boiled Eggs

Fill a medium saucepan — the one with the handle and the higher sides — with water about twice the depth of an egg. Add a few pinches of salt and put it on a hot burner.

While the water is warming up, put ice and water into a medium bowl. Put it to the side.

Once the water is boiling, use a slotted spoon — the big one with holes in it — to carefully lower the eggs into the water. If you drop them, they will crack, and that is no bueno.

Set a timer for six minutes and do nothing until it goes off.

Once the timer goes off, move the pan off the heat and use the slotted spoon to remove the eggs — one at a time — from the hot water. Put them into the bowl of ice water gently. This will stop them from cooking.

While the eggs are cooling, turn your sink water on cold and slowly empty the boiling water down the drain.

After the eggs have sat in the ice bath for two or three minutes, remove them and either a) let them sit or b) crack them open, add some salt and enjoy.

Booyah — you've got breakfast, lunch or a healthy snack for later.

Eggs are cheap and easy to cook. For $15 you can master all three of these techniques, add some skills to your arsenal and never be left hungry.

Liking Someone Means Respecting Them

My son Jack seemed a little nervous before going to bed. He's normally a pretty cool, calm kid, but that night, something was different. His mom told me to go talk to him "man to man." He was 12.

I laid down next to him on the bed and asked if he was nervous about school.

Nope.

Sports?

Nope.

Was it a girl?

Long silence.

After a few minutes, he opened up to me. He liked a girl. He thought maybe she liked him. Earlier that day, his friends were being loud teasing them both during lunch. He was nervous because he had never liked someone before — that I know of — and the whole scene at the lunch table made him worry about going back to school the next day.

His friends had been jerks — like a lot of boys that age — and he worried she felt worried too.

We talked about it and decided that, while he couldn't control his friends, he could control his response. He reached out to her, apologized for embarrassing her and his friends' behavior. Then he told her he liked her.

He had his first girlfriend.

There's a big difference between your friends and the person you like. Your friends need to earn (and keep earning) your respect and honesty. The person you like deserves it.

Liking someone is a crazy experience. It can tie you up inside and lift you higher than you ever thought possible. Your hormones are going crazy, and you're experiencing emotions you don't quite understand. Everyone goes through it — it's not just you.

Talking to your parents about these things is hard. I was lucky that Jack opened up to me because I was able to help that night. It was brave of him to do that. But you may not feel comfortable talking. It's okay. Here's what you need to know:

Who you like is your business, not your friends'. You don't have to tell them.

If you think someone likes you, reach out to them privately — they deserve your honesty.

Your relationship is between the two of you first. Keep it between the two of you. It's not locker room gossip. It's not something to be paraded around.

Like the person enough to respect their feelings. You may talk to a close friend or relative about the relationship as you try and figure things out, but don't disrespect the person by turning them into gossip, a meme or the subject of ridicule.

It's hard. There will be pressure on you to brag or kiss and tell. Don't do it. That's a good way to get dumped and to get the reputation of a guy who can't be trusted.

Like the people you like. Be honest, trustworthy and respectful.

You may get your heart broken a few times, but you'll be the kind of man that people like and respect, which is who you want to be.

Trust me.

❖

Write Letters

When I was 11 years old, I read an article about a guy named Tinker Hatfield. He was a designer at Nike and the lead designer for Air Jordan. Something about his job inspired me, and I really wanted to know more. I began sketching shoes, and when I had a few designs I liked, I put them in an envelope, typed up a letter and sent it off to an address I found on the back of a Nike shoe box.

The most amazing thing happened: He wrote back.

No, he didn't turn any of my designs into shoes, but I was hooked on the rush of going to the mailbox and seeing an envelope with my name on it. I started sending designs to every shoe company I could think of. I kept an address book. I saved the replies, which ranged from "thanks for your interest" letters to free products, tours of offices and, eventually, advice on my career from the owner of Orvis, a company I love to this day.

You are growing up in a world of instantaneous communication. You can reach anyone in the world with the @ symbol. And it's easy to take that access for granted. But don't overlook the value of writing letters on paper and sending them in an envelope.

Doing the work of finding out how to reach someone teaches you skills that will come in handy later in life. Being able to sit down and express yourself in writing will set you apart from all the other kids who are only communicating via text or social media. And there are few things more satisfying than receiving mail with your name on it — for you and for the person to whom you are writing.

Pick someone you admire — an athlete, an actor, a politician, an executive.

Research their address.

Write a letter.

Repeat.

To this day, I still write letters, and I've encouraged boys like you to do the same. Some have reached executives at Under Armour, athletes and TV personalities.

You won't always get a response, but when you do, it's so much more fulfilling than a reply or an @ mention.

❖

People Are Watching

You are being watched. Seriously. Everything you do is seen. Know that and act accordingly.

Your parents and grandparents grew up in a world without devices. They had some, but not like you do. Talking to their friends meant getting on the family phone or climbing on a bike and going to their house. No texting or social media. No cameras or microphones. We were watched by neighbors and parents — like you are — but we could disappear a little.

You can't.

You are being watched through your devices. What you think of as private conversations can be screengrabbed and shared. Your friends' parents are checking their kids' devices. People pretending to be other people are messaging you. Everything you do on your device — even when the app promises that the messages disappear — can be found, shared and return to bite you. Don't put anything into a device you don't want your parents and strangers to know about.

The same thing goes IRL. People are watching. They are watching how you behave at school and on the field, at the movies, walking home, at other people's houses. And there are networks you don't see where your behavior is being seen and shared. Act like a jerk at the high school football game, and someone's mom will see it and call your mom to tell her. You're in trouble before you even get home.

None of this is meant to scare you. It's just that, at your age, it's easy to believe that your actions don't have consequences and that other people don't exist. The sooner you realize that people are always watching and talking about you, the better off you're going to be.

Don't take inappropriate pictures or videos. Don't write nasty things. Don't act like a jerk. People know. And once you get the reputation of being a jerk or being the kid who does inappropriate things with his phone, it will take a very long time for you to overcome it. The easiest way to be liked and respected is to act likable and respectful at all times.

Your friends may think it's cool to send sexual or crude messages. Don't do it. One of their parents is reading those messages.

A guy at school may take pictures of his privates and send it to people because he thinks it's awesome. It is not. At least one of the people who received it was bothered by it — because it's a crime and wrong — and spoke to her mom about it ... and that mom talked to another mom who talked to another. That kid is now a pervert, idiot and criminal. How cool is that?

Don't screen grab people's messages and share them.

Don't make private things public.

Don't be a jerk.

People are always watching.

Open Doors

It's not old fashioned or old school or lame — it's basic manners. Open doors for people. Hold elevators when you see someone coming, and let the people who are already in the elevator out before you go in. This is pretty basic stuff.

Holding the door open, letting other people go in front of you or being considerate and not blasting your music so loud other people can't hear themselves think shows that you understand you are a member of a community and that being a member of a community means recognizing other people.

Your family is a community. Your school. Your church. Your team. Your neighborhood. Even when you are around strangers, you are in a community. Communities are groups of people sharing a common experience — even if it's only for a moment. And good members of the community put others before themselves.

There's nowhere you need to get so urgently that justifies cutting people off or letting a door slam in their face. There's nothing so important that makes it okay to act like you are more important than others.

People notice selfish behavior. They notice courtesy as well. Are you going to be the man who acts selfishly? Or are you going to be the man who shows people you care?

Get in the habit of holding doors open for others. You don't have to stand there all day or not get to where you are going. Just hold the door if someone else is coming. Hold it until another polite person who understands how communities work comes along and takes over. You just might be the best part of someone's bad day. People will thank you and smile. Nod and say, "You're welcome," and feel good about being a good man.

Work for Free

Do you want to make money? Do you want to be successful?

Work for free.

As you're growing up, you're going to need money. Dates, games, food, clothes, a car. There are going to be things you want, and you should earn the money to get them. You'll have jobs you hate for tiny bits of money. I'm not talking about that kind of work. I'm talking about the kind of work that will teach you how to be successful in life.

Start with your chores. A lot of parents will pay for kids to do their chores but understand that payment is an award for your responsibility and contribution. It is not a guarantee or a birthright. You are a member of a family, a household, a community. You have the responsibility to do your share. Don't do it because you're getting paid. Get paid because you do it.

If there's something you want to be doing, don't think about how much you'll get for it. Start doing it and then get paid later. When I was in high school, I wanted to be a reporter. I didn't walk into the local newspaper office and ask for a salary. I walked in and told them I'd write for free if they gave me the opportunity. They did, and I wrote for free for about two weeks before they started paying me … and kept paying me to write while I was in college.

No one is offering me money to write this book. Instead, I'm writing it because I believe in it. I feel compelled to do it. I'll worry about getting paid later. The work I do on this book is meaningful.

There is a difference between a job and meaningful work. Jobs come and go but learning how to do meaningful work will change your life. A job is flipping burgers.

Meaningful work is the work you do because you want to do it — you want to be a part of a family, you want to have good relationships at home, you want to learn how to do something or set your own path. Don't wait for the salary to come before you start pursuing meaningful work.

Start doing the work. Dedicate yourself to doing it. Do it for free, because you won't be doing it for free for long and, who knows, it just might change your life.

❖

Focus on Assists

Do you know why — for me and many other people — LeBron James will go down as a better basketball player than Kobe Bryant? It's not because of his championships. Kobe has more. It's not because of his dunks or his scoring. Kobe was electric at both. It's because when the game was on the line, Kobe wanted to be the one to shoot the ball, and LeBron looked for someone to pass it to.

There's nothing wrong with Kobe's competitiveness, his ability to score or the sense of responsibility he felt for his team's winning. Those are all great things. But what sets LeBron apart, for me, is that he made everyone else on the team around him better. He made them better players, gave them better opportunities, gave them a chance to stand out. LeBron focused as much on his ability to get assists as he did on his ability to score.

I love Kobe. This is not a knock on him. He's a top five all-time player in my mind. But when teammates talk about LeBron, they talk about his ability to see the game happen before it happens, to find the open man. When he was young, he was all about being the superstar, but as he has matured, he is all about being the captain.

In sports and life, you are going to come across a lot of Kobes — superstars who can carry a game on their backs. But try to be like LeBron. Don't try to do it all yourself — even if you can. Instead, try to make everyone else around you better so that you don't have to do it all yourself.

Life, like basketball, is a team sport. Your team is your friends, your family, coworkers and your teammates. Be the kind of player who does his best to be his best but does his best to help others be their best too.

Shake Their Hand, Look Them in the Eye

Meeting new people, particularly meeting adults when you're a kid, is kind of terrifying. They're big. They're old. You don't know what to say. People will forgive you for being a little sheepish. But if you do it right, they'll remember you for it.

Here's how to meet people — adults, teachers, coaches, students, friends, whomever.

Extend your right hand for a shake. Lead with the thumb and point your fingers toward their feet. This will prevent that weird, floppy fish kind of handshake that is awkward for everyone.

Look them in the eye. Not at their chest, their belt, their shoes, the wall or anywhere else. But try not to look directly into their eyes. Instead, look at the space right between their eyes where their forehead, eyes and nose meet.

Introduce yourself. Say, "Nice to meet you. I'm (first name) (last name)." You have to say something. Don't make it harder than it needs to be. Keep it simple. Nice to meet you and your name. No matter how nervous they make you feel, you can remember this much. If you have already met them, say, "Nice to see you again (Mr. or Mrs. or Ms.) (last name)."

Again, keep it simple.

Let them let go first. Don't pull your hand away. Be firm but not stiff. Hold on until they let go. Keep looking at the space above their nose and between their eyes. When they look away, you look away.

Done and done. It's simple but important. If you learn to meet people this way when you're young, you'll keep doing it when it really matters and when people will be judging you.

In review:

Lead with the thumb. Look them between the eyes. Speak confidently. Let them let go first and look away when they do.

❖

Know How to Swear

Any idiot can use foul language. What makes a man different is his understanding of the right time to curse and the wrong time to curse.

Your parents aren't stupid. They know you're learning bad language. You hear it on the bus, in the hallways, the locker room, when you're with your friends and in music, movies and games. We learned bad language the same way. Yes, contrary to what you might believe, we were kids once too, and learning swear words was a rite of passage. The same goes for your grandparents, great-grandparents and every adult you know.

So, let's put that behind us. Your parents know how to swear, and they know that you know bad words too. What does it mean to learn how to swear?

It's all about the audience and context. Know who you are around. Know where you are. Know what devices are being pointed in your direction. Here are a few rules to swear by:

1. If there is an adult around, don't swear. Coaches, teachers, clergy, bosses, your friends' parents, grandparents, whoever. Your parents may let you get away

with it but go easy there because they want to believe you are a good kid at heart.

2. If you are in school, church, at your job, on the bus or in front of people you don't know, don't swear.

3. If you are around romantic interests, girls, people who don't know you well, don't swear.

4. If someone is recording you, don't swear.

5. If you are on a group text, social media or live gaming, don't swear.

Swearing is not just using bad words, but also being willfully inappropriate, sexual or just plain disgusting. There are times when swearing is fine. It can even be appropriate.

If you're building something and smack your hand with a hammer — go ahead, let one fly.

If you're walking through the woods and suddenly notice you are being stalked by a blood-thirsty bear, by all means.

If you're with your friends and telling jokes, as long as they aren't posting videos for the world to see, fine.

But don't mistake learning swear words with learning how to swear. Swearing is easy but swearing properly requires situational awareness.

Carry Their Groceries, Not Their Baggage

Some people need help. They need help carrying something or doing some chores. They need help for a moment or on a longer-term project.

Help them. Be a helpful kid. Be a helpful man. But know the difference between helping someone do something and fixing their lives.

You can help a friend who is struggling with some homework that you understand, but you can't do his work for him.

You can help your parents do some work around the house, but you can't fix their marriage.

You can be kind to a love interest and listen to them when they are stressed out, but you can't make them happy if they aren't.

You will have an instinct or inkling to try and fix things for other people. Don't do it. Be a helper, not a fixer. Helpers make other people's lives easier or better for a moment, but fixers can drive themselves crazy and make themselves miserable trying to do too much for other people. They can lose sight of their own needs by putting others ahead of their own.

Do not be afraid to be a helper. If you see someone struggling to carry their groceries, by all means, go grab some bags. But if you see someone struggling with their emotional or psychological baggage, steer clear.

It won't make sense right away, but over time, it will.

Leave No Trace

If you've ever been camping or have been in the Scouts, you've probably heard the phrase "leave no trace." It means to clean up after yourself. Clean up your trash. Put your things away. Leave the place you were as good or better than when you got there.

It's a good rule of thumb for your life as well and means that you don't leave things for other people to deal with.

Do your dishes. Pick up your room. Hang up your towel. Clean up your desk. Don't leave anything behind. Don't leave a mess.

There are very few places in your life that are yours and yours alone. Your bedroom belongs to your parents. Your locker, your desk, the locker room belong to the school. Campgrounds, parks and ball fields belong to everyone who uses them. Don't be the guy who makes other people clean up after you before they can enjoy or use the place you just used.

It's not a chore or work; it's basic responsibility and good practice for your youth and the rest of your life.

Leave no trace at home and other people's houses.

Leave no trace at school, on the bus or in the locker room.

Leave no trace in public places, parks, stadiums and movie theaters.

If you brought something in with you, take it out with you.

Leave no trace. It makes a big difference.

Own Up to It and Apologize

Put simply: Make amends, not excuses.

Everybody screws up. Everybody makes mistakes. Everybody does something they shouldn't or doesn't do something they should. It's human, and no matter how perfect you try to be, you are a member of the species as well.

What distinguishes a man from a guy is that a man owns up to his mistakes and tries to make amends by apologizing, learning and moving on.

No one expects you to be perfect (except maybe you). Your parents, your teachers, your friends — they like you. They don't need you to be a super human. They just need you to be you.

When you screw up, admit it. Don't blame other things or people. Don't make excuses. Don't try to downplay the impact your mistake had on other people, but don't overplay it either. Just acknowledge what you did wrong — or what you didn't do — apologize for it and move on.

It can seem pretty scary. I remember when I was 16, I got into a minor car accident driving my dad's car. I was terrified the whole way home. I tried coming up with excuses that would make the accident someone else's fault. I imagined the worst possible outcome — would I lose my driver's license? Would my dad hate me? I broke out in a watery sweat when I pulled into my neighborhood.

I parked the car and was still trying to figure out a way that the accident wasn't my fault when I walked around the house and found my dad in the backyard. I thought about leaving, but he saw me and approached me, and I knew that I was out of time.

"I had an accident," I told him. "I backed into a parked car. I am so sorry."

A micro-second felt like an hour as I waited for his wrath but guess what. It never came. He asked me if I was okay, thanked me for owning up to it and taught me how to deal with the insurance company to fix the car. He told me I did the right thing, and the whole thing was over in seconds.

Had I made up an excuse or lied, I would probably still be in trouble. My relationship with my dad might not be what it is today. But instead, because I owned up to it, apologized, fixed it and learned from it, I like to think it brought us closer.

You are going to make mistakes. It's not the mistakes that define who you are, but what you do after. Be the person who other people want to forgive and help out. Don't make excuses. Just apologize and move on.

Let Your Game Do the Talking

The guys who are good sometimes talk about it all the time. The guys who are good all the time don't say a word. They let their games do the talking.

You know that feeling when someone on the other team does something good — drives in a run, makes a catch, drains a three — and then gets up in your face to make sure you understand what he just did? You want to punch him in the face … until he strikes out, drops the ball or throws up an airball. Then you just want to laugh at him. Why? Because he made a huge deal out of a small success.

Do you know who doesn't do that? The guys who expect to drive in the runs, make the catches and drain the threes. They have devoted huge portions of their lives to become good at those things. The truly great don't need to say a word. They hit the gym, they hit the books, they stay after practice and do extra credit. People know they are great because they stand out through their greatness, not their words.

Their greatness is based on the fact that they realize they can always be better. It was just one at-bat, one catch, one three-pointer, and they want to do that thousands of times over the course of their careers. They realize success is an event, and so is failure. Greatness in anything is never defined by an event, but a lifelong pursuit, a dedication and determination to be better tomorrow than today. They know they will get better every time they hit the field or the court because they do the work to make sure of it.

It's okay to be excited about a good play. Pump your first. High five your teammates. Nod to your mom in the stands. But don't let that excitement turn into trash talk or acting like a jerk — it will only come back to haunt you. Instead, focus on the next play, because the next play is always the one that matters.

Do Your Chores

Do your chores.

Not because you get paid. Not because your parents told you to. Not because you're trying to kiss up. Not because you want to and not because they are easy.

Do them because you don't want to. Do them because they are hard or are a pain. Do them because there are a lot of other things you'd rather be doing.

Doing your chores is about learning responsibility and contributing to the workload required to keep a house and family running. But even more than that, doing your chores is about learning how to make room in your life for things you don't want to do. Doing your chores prepares you for your future life where, the older you get, the less it will be made up of activities you are excited about doing. The sooner you learn that the easier your transition to that future will be.

Ask any adult what they do regularly that they'd rather not do, and they will have a list. Paying bills. Commuting to work. Fixing the house. Taxes. There are hundreds of things adults do because they have to, things they wish weren't part of being an adult. But we've learned to do these things and doing them makes the things we want to do even better.

Ever wonder why your dad seems to love sitting on the couch watching a game or a movie? It's because he's run around all day doing a bunch of things he didn't want to do so that he COULD sit on the couch and watch the game. What about your mom? Ever wonder why she seems to get so excited to do something as a family? It's because she's busted her hump to make sure the family would be able to spend time together.

If you fill these growing up years only doing the things you want to do, the transition to adult responsibilities will be miserable. It will be like tearing all the hair off your head with duct tape. But if you do your chores and learn to do things you don't want to do a little bit over time, it won't be so bad, and you'll be able to focus not on the chores of adulthood, but on enjoying the good stuff.

So, do your chores. Complain to yourself, but not to your parents, and know that the task is making you a better person. Your family will appreciate it.

If life were all pool parties and championship games, neither of those things would matter. Instead, tackling the difficult or crappy head-on will make the good stuff that much better.

❖

Look Up Every Once in a While

The next time you're out shopping or walking down a busy street, look around. You'll see a lot of people with their heads down, earbuds in, fingers tapping away at their phones. They look like ghosts in reverse. Their bodies are present, but their minds, spirits and souls are someplace else. This is what you look like when your nose is down and you're here, but you're gone: a ghost in reverse.

There's nothing wrong with technology. It's important. It's fundamentally changed the world. It's made the world better, smaller and, if you forget to look up every once in a while, a lot lonelier than it needs to be.

That device you carry around gives you access to, quite literally, the entire world. Media, information, entertainment, communications. I wish you were my age, so you could remember what life was like before iPhones, because only then would you be able to appreciate how incredible they are. You can create your own world with a couple of taps on a screen.

That's why smartphones are so addictive and why everyone walks around with their heads down. The problem comes when you only look down and miss the world you actually live in.

Learn to see other people, not their profiles.

Discover things on accident, not through a search.

Make eye contact with people, don't just connect.

Listen to the sounds around you, not just your playlists.

Pay attention, learn and experience life outside the screen.

Be a Student of the Game

If you want to play a game, know the game. If you want to play baseball, watch baseball, read books about baseball, dive deep into baseball. If basketball is your game, know its history and the players who made it. Guys who are great at lacrosse love lacrosse.

It may seem like a silly waste of time — like homework no teacher is ever going to grade — but it makes a big difference. There's a lot that you can learn about the future from the past.

Part of it is passion, and another part is context. The more you know about a game, the more you'll love playing it. The bigger part something plays in your life, the more important it becomes to you.

One of my all-time favorite television characters was a grumpy guy from Indiana named Ron Swanson on the show "Parks and Recreation." He was a simple man of simple principles. He believed in right and wrong and spoke in short, meaningful nuggets of advice. In one episode, an employee of his was struggling to balance her work life and a run for political office. He urged her to quit her job to focus on politics. His reason?

"Never half-ass two things. Whole-ass one thing."

Sorry for the language, but his point is important. You don't have to pick one sport. I'm a big believer in playing multiple sports. But you do need to commit yourself. Not just your body and your time. Commit your brain and your energy. Don't be a skipping stone, bouncing from one thing to the next. Or, rather, do be that, but pick a couple of things and go deep.

Be a student of the game.

❖

Know What's No One Else's Business

One of the hardest things to learn to say is nothing at all. It's hard to know what to tell other people about yourself. It's easier with your family and your best friends. It's harder with people you kind of know or have just met. But, there are some things you are better off not talking about at all.

Don't talk about the details of your relationships with significant others, particularly your physical relationships. Your sex life is between you and your partner, and your friends should have nothing to do with it. If you have questions, talk to your parents. Talk to your partner — the other person in the relationship. Bragging to your friends only ends up badly. You will embarrass your partner, and they will resent you for it. You may think you're cool, but you actually are just a jerk. If someone is abusing you, find an adult you trust and run to them. If you have questions, same thing. Your friends don't know anything, nor should they.

Don't talk about your grades or achievements. Unless it's with a study partner, a counselor or a coach. No one wants to hear you brag if you're doing great.

And if you're struggling, the only people you should be talking to are the people who can and will help you.

Don't talk about money. It's just a sticky subject. You're better off talking to your parents about it. But money and religion are topics that can make other people uncomfortable and make you seem like the guy who only wants to talk about money or religion.

The point isn't to avoid topics — it's to think about the consequences of your words. If they can hurt people you care about, don't say them. If they can lead to people thinking you are something you are not, keep your mouth shut.

You can be interesting without being hurtful. You can stand out by asking questions. You can make an impression by being the person who knows what other people should know and what they shouldn't.

And if you're not sure, if you have a little voice in the back of your head that wonders whether or not you should share something, you're probably better off listening to it.

❖

Be Gracious, Not Right

The single most annoying word in the English language is actually. It's not always annoying, but there is a circumstance when it's worse than the sound of nails on a chalkboard.

What is that circumstance?

Let me paint a picture here with some other words.

You're with a group of friends. You're laughing and joking, having the time of your life. Somebody says something hilarious, and the entire group nearly spews soda out of their noses ... except for one guy. He's the guy who knows everything. He thinks he's smarter than you, and he always wants to prove it. He starts to speak: "Actually ..." In seconds the laughter stops. The momentum is gone. The moment is dead all because some jerk needed to correct people at a time when being correct was not important in the least.

I hate that guy. I hate it when I am that guy. I hate it when I or other people put their insane need to be correct above the moment. I'm guessing you hate it too.

There's no hard and true rule to knowing when being right matters. It's a feeling, not an absolute. You'll have to live and learn and experiment a bit, but it's worth it. Even though there are no hard rules, there are some moments you can look for to try out not being a know-it-all.

If an adult is going on and on about politics over family dinner, don't argue with them. You won't change their mind and will just end up stress-eating leftover Thanksgiving stuffing.

If there's no value in being right, if there's no money on the line and no consequences to you or the people you really care about, let it go.

If being right is the thing that's going to derail a moment, keep the experience going. Let the facts slide.

There's an old saying: "Discretion is the better part of valor." It's a confusing sentence, but it basically means that knowing when to act — and when not to act — is the most important thing a hero can do.

It's the same with being right. Knowing when to double down on being right and when to let it go may just be the most correct thing you can do.

❖

Be a Good Guest

A personal hero of mine is the chef, traveler, author, TV host and entrepreneur Anthony Bourdain. He died in the summer of 2018 after nearly 20 years of making the best television I have ever seen and writing some of my all-time favorite books. In his work, he dined with presidents and peasants, visited paradises and war zones and ate the most innovative and simplest food on the planet. He made ordinary people of all kinds interesting to millions and proved that despite our differences, most people in the world want the same things: peace, family, love and a good meal.

I learned a lot from Anthony Bourdain without ever having a conversation with him. I learned about traveling and cultures around the world; I learned about food and writing. But the best lesson I ever learned from this man who captivated the first half of my adulthood was this: Be a good guest.

What does that mean?

It means eating something that someone made for you, whether you think you'll like it or not because it is a gift.

It means respecting the culture, values and norms of the place you are visiting, not arguing with the people there or thinking you are superior to them.

It means asking questions and listening to people and participating in the conversation, being curious about people and learning from them, not just talking at them.

It means doing the dishes, staying late to help clean up and respecting other people's homes, cities and countries. Japanese soccer fans are famous for staying after games to clean up the stadium, whether their team is the host or visitor, whether they won or lost.

Being a good guest, when you're growing up, means talking to your friends' parents and clearing your plate. It means respecting their house, their furniture and their possessions by not breaking them, spilling on them, jumping on them or otherwise treating them disrespectfully. It means eating the meatloaf, even if you don't like meatloaf. It means taking care of the team equipment and leaving the gym cleaner than you found it. It means listening to the teacher and respecting the school. It means respecting people's time, effort and care by saying thank you, being on time and looking them in the eye.

Be a good guest, and you'll be welcomed back. Don't, and your reputation will precede you.

❖

Be a Good Host

There are two sides to being a good host: taking care of your guests and taking care of your family and house.

Having friends over is awesome. It's fun to go to other people's houses, but having your buddies and, eventually, romantic interest over for a movie date. It's comforting to be in your own place, but being a host comes with some responsibilities.

It's your job — not your mom's — to make sure your guests are comfortable, fed, have something to drink and know where the bathroom is.

It's your job to make them feel welcome and comfortable with your family. Introduce them. Spend a few minutes chatting with your family before disappearing to the basement or your room or wherever you want to go.

It's your job to make sure your guests are being good guests. That means if the house rule is no eating on the couch, you ask your friends — nicely — not to eat on the couch. You have to set the tone for how your guests are expected to respect your house. You, not they, will be held accountable if anything is broken, ripped, torn or stained. Take care of it.

Let your guest go first. If you're playing a game, walking through a doorway, using the restroom, let them go first. It is what hosts are supposed to do.

Be prepared to suggest things to do. Don't make your guests come up with ideas. They don't always know what you have. Pre-select some movies, games or activities. Suggest them to get the ball rolling.

Don't turn having people over as an invitation to act like a jerk. Everybody, but especially boys your age, feels a need to show off in front of their friends. This doesn't give you the right to be mean to your siblings, abuse the family pet or speak disrespectfully to your parents. If anything, you need to be nicer and more patient to your family and pets when your friends are around than when they are not. How you treat the people sharing your house reflects on more than just you — it reflects on your family and how your guests will think of them after they are gone.

Don't take any of these tips as a reason not to host. Have people over, but keep in mind that you are not just a participant, you are the host. Be a good one.

❖

Know Some Jokes and Stories

It might seem silly, but you should learn some jokes. You never know when they are going to come in handy.

As you grow up, you're going to find yourself in all kinds of weird social situations. Being able to tell a joke or two or a few good stories will make awkward moments a whole lot easier. Like putting oil on your bike chain, a decent joke can get the conversation moving a whole lot smoother and easier.

Here are a couple that I like to have handy. (Warning: They are a little corny, but they are friendly for all audiences. Also, I don't know who wrote these and don't claim they are original.)

The Bear

A grizzly bear was walking down the street and realized he was thirsty. He looked across the street, saw a bar and decided to go inside. He walked up to the bar and sat down on a stool.

The bartender asked him, "What will it be?"

"I'll have a … … … beer," the bear said.

"Why the big pause?" The bartender asked.

The grizzly bear said, "I was born with them."

Get it? Okay, not great but good enough to get things started. Here's another one.

The Wizard

What do you call a 100-year-old wizard who walks everywhere with no shoes on and has really bad breath?

"A super-calloused fragile mystic with chronic halitosis."

Learn some jokes. It will make you popular at parties.

Root for Other People

Everybody likes to hear people cheering for them. Every boy dreams of being the athlete with the ball in his hand when the game is on the line, the crowd chanting his name.

Not a lot of us dream about being the guy in the stands doing the chanting, but we absolutely should be.

If you want fans, be a fan. If you want your friends and family or that cute girl from science class to show up for your big moments on the court or the field, you should show up for theirs.

It's that simple.

Make the effort to go to your best friend's game. Show up at your sister's concert. Dress up. Bring her flowers. Put your phone away. Pay attention. Clap loudly.

Being rooted for feels great and is easy. If you want to show someone you appreciate them, don't just point to them in the stands — put your butt in the stands when it's their turn.

You'll make them feel great. You'll probably have a blast and, importantly, you'll make someone else's dream of stepping into the light and having the crowd go wild come true.

Read the Plaque

There's a plaque on the outside wall of a house in London that says, "The American Patriot" Benedict Arnold lived there from the time he moved to the city until he died. American patriot? Isn't he the guy famous for selling the Americans out to the British during the Revolutionary War?

There's a plaque in rural western Ohio that marks the place where sharpshooter Annie Oakley was buried.

There's a bronze plaque in the floor of the Mall of America that marks the placement and orientation of home plate in the old Minnesota Twins stadium.

There's a plaque embedded on the landing of the Lincoln Memorial that marks the exact spot where Dr. Martin Luther King stood while delivering his "I Have a Dream" speech, one of the most famous in history.

There's something incredible about walking down the street and realizing, very suddenly, that's you are someplace where something significant happened. It's interesting, sometimes exciting and usually pretty cool.

History, when you read about it in books, can be boring. It can be stuffy and seem a million miles away from your life. But when you're out in the world and literally standing on the spot where something happened, history becomes real. Real people did real things in real places — the same place you are standing.

Not everybody needs to be a historian, but learning in the real world connects you to it. Read the plaque, look around, learn stuff just for fun.

Commit ... Even if You're Not Ready

There is nothing more valuable in a person than commitment. A person who commits to things is a person who can be trusted, a person you can rely on. Commitments are promises you make to other people and yourself.

When you join a team, commit to it. That means you show up every practice and game ready to work. You work hard even when it looks like the game is a loss. You listen to and respect your coaches and teammates. You are a player your team can count on and see the season through, no matter what.

When you commit to a job, you show up on time, ready to work. You don't come in late or not show up. You are there and reliable. You made that promise.

When you commit to a relationship, you make it a priority. You are honest and open. You make the other person feel valued, even when things are going badly. You put that person ahead of others and make them the priority. You should be their priority as well. If you're not, it's time to move on.

If you tell someone you'll be somewhere, be there. If you say you're going to do something, do it. Don't make excuses. Don't make up reasons. Just get it done. Give it everything you've got. If at the end of the season you want to switch teams, you can. But the second you join a team, be part of the team no matter what.

Be on Time

It's pretty simple: If you say you're going to be somewhere at a certain time, be there. If something starts at a certain time, be there early.

Punctuality becomes pretty fluid as you get older. There are no school bells that ring for you to show up at work. There is no threat of being tardy if you blow through your curfew. But don't mistake a lack of reminders for a lack of consequences.

Practice, games, church — be 10 or 15 minutes early. A lot of times, you will have to rely on other people — siblings, parents, friends and friends' parents — for a ride. Don't make them wait. Be at the field or on the court ready, with your shoes tied and your gear prepared before the coach tells you to start warming up. Get to church early to get a pew and spend a little time settling in before the service starts. That way, you won't disturb other people who were on time and want to participate in the service.

Curfew, dates, parties and social functions — be on time. Don't show up early for a date; the person you are taking out might not be ready. Don't be early for a party for the same reason. But don't think it's cool to be "fashionably late" because it's not — especially if there is food involved. The host has been hustling to have everything ready, and they will probably wait around for you to arrive before eating. While they are waiting, they will see all their effort to prepare a well-crafted and hot meal go to waste because you couldn't get moving. Don't be late for curfew because your parents — no matter what you think, or what they say — are sitting up worried about you.

Work, meetings, appointments — be on time and communicate if you won't be. Leaving people waiting is rude and will make you look like a slacker who doesn't care. Even if your job is flipping burgers, the manager cares. They notice your effort and your hustle the same way they notice the quality of food.

Being on time is more than just being punctual. It's a sign of your consideration for other people and their time; it's an indication of your reliability and shows people that you are someone who can be trusted.

Don't leave people waiting. Be on time.

Dress for the Moment

I get it — sweats pants and sneakers are comfortable. Flip flops are a lot easier to wear than shoes, and we don't live in the 1950s when men put on suits to check the mailbox. Our world is pretty casual and, as a young man, the idea of dressing up is pretty lame.

But sometimes, you've got to dress for the occasion.

You may think dressing a certain way is an expression of your personal brand, your style, your personality. And you're right. But you can't ignore the context in which you are wearing things. The clothes need to match the man and the moment.

Don't dress like you're going to basketball practice when you're going to a funeral or a fancy dinner. Don't dress like you're lounging around the house on a Saturday morning when you're going on a job interview or to church. Put on some nice pants and a button-down shirt. Comb your hair. Look like you care about where you are going.

I'm not saying you always have to be dressy. You don't. Imagine someone wearing pressed pants, a sports coat and bow tie and showing up to run in a track meet. They would look pretty stupid, right? They would look like they have no idea where they are or what they are doing.

You look just as stupid when you arrive to pick up your date wearing pajama pants and slippers. You look just a dumb when you wear basketball shorts, a jersey and a ratty cap to your sister's graduation party.

How you dress is the first thing people notice about you. It's like a visual handshake before you even open your mouth. You are free to dress how you like most of the time, but be aware of the situations that call for you to step up your game and wear something nice.

Your mom will be so proud, and everyone else will notice.

Read a Book

Read this book. Read one of my other ones. Read "Hatchet" by Gary Paulsen. Read Douglas Adams' "The Hitchhiker's Guide to the Galaxy." Read the "Hunger Games" trilogy or the "Maze Runner" books. Read a biography of Jackie Robinson or the history of basket-weaving. It doesn't matter what the book is, just read it.

Don't do it for homework — but if you have reading to do for homework, you should ABSOLUTELY do it. Don't do it because your mom tells you — but if she asks you to read, listen to her.

Read because reading makes you smarter — it does. Read because you'll get more out of it than TV — you will. Read because it's a better escape from the real world that any amount of social media or gaming ever could be. Read because you'll be a better, more complete, more considered and likable person.

You can read websites or magazines, but nothing replaces a book. There is a unique kind of anticipation and fulfillment when you close in on the end of the book and eventually turn the last page.

Read books. Do it every day. Always have a book going.

Do it.

Ask for Help

As you grow up, talking to your parents about the things that bother you will get harder and harder. There's something about the flood of hormones, the change in how your life works, the pressure from your friends that makes you clam up when you should be talking the most. You start to feel like you should be able to fix everything yourself or pretend like nothing's bothering you.

There's nothing dumber than that kind of pride.

Seriously. Nothing dumber.

You may not believe it, but your parents can be really helpful. They've been there. They were your age once and went through things very similar things to what you're going through. They know more than you give them credit for, and they have your back.

They want to help. They have helped you your entire life. They live to help you. It's part of their lives. It makes them feel good. Let them help.

Still not convinced?

Try your friends, your teachers, your friends' parents, your siblings. Call your grandparents, your doctor, your coach.

You are never as alone as you think you are. Don't be too proud or afraid to ask for the help you need, even if you're not sure what you're asking for.

Ask Questions and Listen to the Answers

My friend David asks amazing questions. Every time I'm around him, he asks about me, my work, my life, my world. He doesn't ask so that he can answer. He asks because he wants to hear what I have to say.

It makes me want to be around him more.

A lot of boys talk about themselves. A lot of men do it too. They talk about themselves because they're arrogant or because they are nervous — either way, they are not secure enough with themselves to allow conversations to be about other people.

David hasn't always been a good question asker. He used to be just like all the rest of the insecure self-talkers, but one day he just got tired of talking about himself. He met someone interesting and found himself trying so hard to impress that person that he missed the opportunity to learn anything about them. He knew he needed to change, so he developed a system.

Every morning when David gets up, he puts five pennies in his right pants pocket. Every time he stops to talk to someone and asks them a question, he moves a penny into his left pocket. He won't go home until he's moved all of his pennies.

The amazing result of this simple system is that he knows people around him a lot better than anyone else does. He understands the people in his life. He learns from them. They trust him. They like him. He cares for them, and they know it. But, most amazingly, he doesn't feel like he has to be the one talking anymore. He doesn't feel the pressure to make himself sound so cool. He can just be himself and being himself means asking questions.

Ask questions. Ask your friends about their days and listen to the answers. Ask your siblings about their dreams and listen to what they have to say. Ask your teachers where they went to college. Ask your coaches where they learned to play.

People aren't so scary when you talk to them. And asking questions will help you understand your world. Put some pennies in your pockets and ask about the world. It might be hard at first, but before you know it, you'll end up smarter, calmer and more invested in your world.

❖

Don't Be a Frontrunner

Everyone likes a winner, but there are people out there who only like winners. You know the kids. They're the ones who show up with the jersey of the latest championship-winning team and claim, despite all evidence, that they've been a lifelong, die-hard fan of that team, which is based in a city they've never been to or lived in, and plays a sport in which they have never shown any interest.

These are front runners. Don't be a front runner.

You don't have to only root for the teams closest to where you live, but a personal connection will make being a fan a whole lot better.

In the 1990s, there were kids everywhere who claimed a lifelong love of the Chicago Bulls. I was one of them. But I really was a fan of Michael Jordan — or, at least, the idea of Michael Jordan. My fandom of the Bulls ended when he retired for good. It wasn't until later that I realized the value of rooting for my local teams, no matter the outcome.

We tend to think of sports as games or entertainment, and they are. But hidden in the experience of being a sports fan is the opportunity to learn about yourself — who you are, the person you will become, the kind of man you want to be. How you react to winning and losing, how you handle adversity, how you cope with upset and celebrate with grace — all these things will be important to shaping the man you will become.

And all of them start with loyalty.

If you only root for winners, you don't know the joy of overcoming defeat.

If you only root for superstars, you don't learn about the value of hard work and dedication.

If you jump from team to team based on their winning records, you don't develop the integrity that will get you hired, promoted, loved and trusted.

Front runners are the worst kinds of fans. They are arrogant without ability, self-righteous without reason and annoying to everyone around them.

Don't be a front runner. Pick a team and stick with them through thick and thin, good seasons and bad.

❖

Unplug and Go

Sometimes you just have to go.

Go for a walk. Go lay in a hammock in the backyard. Go ride your bike.

Put your phone away and turn off your screens. Don't have a plan or a schedule. Don't have a purpose. Just tell your mom where you'll be and when you'll be home, then go.

Kids these days live insanely regimented lives. Every moment is planned with activities, from homework to sports to arranged hangouts with family and friends to clubs, activities and extra-curricular classes. Add on constant digital communication and stimulus, and it's enough to drive a kid crazy.

Sometimes you need to just unplug. Wander around the neighborhood or lay in the yard and listen to the birds.

Our brains were not designed for constant stimulus. Our basic nature is to explore. Our bodies were not meant to be constantly busy. Our emotions need a break or else we become broken.

When I was young, I was a latchkey kid. I was home alone after school. I used to wander around in the woods behind my house or sit on the green electrical box in the front yard. I would ride my bike on a circuit around the neighborhood for the sake of riding my bike. Looking back, I had great friends, and I loved playing sports, but the defining moments of my youth were the ones when I unplugged.

There was freedom in it, independence. I — and probably your parents too — worry that your generation is losing that experience. We are probably scheduling your life too much, putting too much pressure on you to succeed in school, sports and other activities.

Make time for just you. Be a little bored. Being bored is not a punishment, it's a release. Wander, roam, smell the roses. Do whatever you want, but don't do it in front of a screen. Try a half-hour a week. Be alone and carefree. Be independent and refreshed.

Looking back, you're not going to cherish busy schedules and Snapchats. You won't remember any of the video games you play. But you will remember the time you walked across your town for fun. You will remember the feeling of lying in the hammock, your skin getting warm in the sun. You'll remember the times you just let go for a little while and how it helped you when you got back.

❖

Love Your Siblings

No one will make you madder than your siblings.

Growing up, there were times I was so mad at my sisters that I would shake and scream curse words into my pillow. I see it in my oldest sons. No one can get to Dylan the way Jack can, and the same goes the other way. They yell at each other. They push and shove and, someday, I think it will come to punches.

You get mad at your siblings because you can. You know each other so well that you feel jealous over nothing and angry over the slightest thing. Your siblings can get to you in a way almost no one else can or ever will.

Love them anyway.

Someday, your parents will be gone. Your friends will come and go, they will move away, or you may grow apart. But your siblings? They are with you forever.

As you get older, you'll come to appreciate the things that make you mad now. They know you for who you are. They have shared a bedroom, a bathroom, a backseat with you. You've been on the same vacations, eaten the same awkward holiday dinners. And while they may have driven you crazy, they understand you in a way no one else ever can.

Take care of those relationships. If you fight, make up. If you hurt them, apologize. Tell them you love them. Answer them when they call. Call them just because.

Like it or not, you're stuck with them, and, eventually, you'll be glad you are.

Play Defense

Offense gets attention, but defense wins championships.

Or something like that. It's an old saying — something one of my coaches used to say. I don't remember exactly how it goes, but the idea is important.

Look, I get it. In almost all instances, defense sucks. It's hard. It's exhausting. But you'll never be the best player on the court or field if you don't play defense.

Michael Jordan came into the league in the 1980s and quickly became one of the most important players ever to pick up a ball. What he could do on offense left the stuffy old guard of the NBA slack-jawed. He seemed to be able to score at will, and some people recognized almost right away that he was going to be one of the best of all time.

Why didn't everyone agree?

Because he didn't play defense. Not really, anyway. That was the criticism that followed a young MJ around the league. Amazing offensive player, but his defense is lazy.

Being the champion that he is, Jordan doubled down. He worked hard on his defense and eventually went on to win the Defensive Player of the Year award.

It's a nice story. But there's a pretty good chance that even if he hadn't focused on his D, Jordan would still be on the Mount Rushmore of Basketball. (No, there is no Mount Rushmore of Basketball, but there totally should be.)

Why bring it up? Because defense is super important. Jordan would not have settled for being an incomplete player. His will to win is legendary, and if there was a hole in his game, he was going to fix it.

But what if you're not a once-in-a-generation offensive force? Does it still matter? More than ever.

Defense is all about focus and effort; it's about hustle and being willing to outwork the guy on the other side of the ball. There will always be people who are better at offense than you. Just know that. But the only thing stopping you from being from standing out on defense sits between your ears and behind your eyes: your brain.

Defense is about mental toughness. It's about never giving up no matter how good the guy you're guarding is or how badly he burned you. He may have gotten the first step, but you can chase him down for the block. He may have gotten behind you, but you should still try and chase him down before he crosses the goal line. The ball may look like it's over the fence, but you should still go up and try to get it.

You may not have the chops to score at will, but there will always be a place in the lineup for the guy who gives his all on D.

Trying and Sucking Beats Not Trying at All

Everybody likes to be good at things. It's not just you or the guy who seems to be good at every sport. It feels good to be good and even better to be great.

But don't let wanting to be good at things stop you from trying things at which you might be bad.

Confused?

Okay, I grew up with a kid who was incredible at golf. From a young age, he could hit a golf ball like nobody's business. Every time I went with him to the driving range or, God forbid, out to play nine, it was clear that as good as he was, I was equally as terrible. After about three times playing with him, I wanted to quit. I never wanted to touch a golf club again. I was bad at it and didn't think I would ever be good enough to even carry his bag.

But I didn't quit. I kept playing and, 30 years later, I've only gotten slightly better. He went on to play college golf and win championships as an adult amateur. I still sometimes leave clubs behind and spend more time in the woods trying to find my ball than hoisting trophies over my head.

Why does it matter? Because, if I had quit, I never would have played rounds with my dad and my sons. I never would have had fun with other friends and never would have found the stress relief of hitting a bucket of balls with my daughter.

If I had quit golf, I would have quit everything I wasn't immediately good at — tennis, music, writing, being a husband and a father — which grew into things I not only loved but became really good at doing.

Try things. Suck at them. Enjoy being bad. Be the kind of kid who learns how to fail. Become the kind of man who is not afraid of taking a risk and doesn't mind not being the best at everything. Take some pressure off yourself and enjoy the experience of trying.

Trying things is how you'll find the things you love, the things that make your life rich. But if you're too afraid of being bad to try, you'll never know what you're missing.

❖

Laughs Are Cheap and Can Cost You

Being funny is awesome. Sacrificing someone else's feelings for the sake of a cheap joke? Not so much.

Every young man I know likes being funny. They like making their friends laugh. It makes them feel liked and accepted. I know it made me feel that way. But funny and mean are separated by a very thin line. And what might be hysterical to you might make someone else feel like garbage, particularly if your brand of humor relies on making fun of others.

This isn't about toughening up or other people being too soft. It's about recognizing the difference good-spirited ribbing — which usually goes both ways — and being a mean-spirited jerk.

Boys and men have an almost genetic instinct to rag on each other. But you have to know when enough is enough. Someone may say they are fine, but are they? Are you being inclusive, or are you being a bully?

No one can really know what other people are feeling. It's impossible to really understand other people's experiences. So, when you go for a joke, make sure it's from a place of respect, not superiority. Be funny, but be willing to take it as much as you give it. And if you don't think you'd say something to someone if your buddies weren't around, don't say it.

You will have an urge to show off your wit. Fine. But show off your intelligence too, and know the difference between friendly bagging and dirt bagging.

If someone is usually the butt of jokes, don't pile on. Be strong enough to stand up to the jokers and say enough is enough.

If someone seems bothered, they probably are. Be man enough to reach out to them and make sure they are okay.

Because one day, you'll be my age, and when you think back, you won't be thinking back at all your zesty one-liners. You'll think back to the times you went too far. You'll remember the times you allowed peer pressure to make you cruel, the times you didn't stand up for someone who needed it.

Funny is great, but it's temporary. Cruelty lasts a lot longer — for the person you were cruel to and for you.

❖

Save Up for Something You Want

If there is one thing I wish I had learned to do as a kid, it would be to have learned how to save better. There were things I put money away for — Air Jordans, a new bike — but not enough. I would work to earn money but spend it too easily and too soon. I had to learn to save as an adult, and it sucked.

So, this one is a little less philosophical and more practical. Pick something you want. Make it expensive and save up for it. You don't have to save every penny you make, but put away a portion of it. See how long it takes to get the thing you want by saving for it.

Let's say a gaming console sells for $500 and you get $10 a week for allowance. You also mow two lawns every week for $20 each. That's $50 a week in income. Pretty good for a kid your age.

The console is $500, but you'll also need at least one game, which will cost another $50. So, if you saved every penny you earn in allowance and mowing money, it would take you 11 weeks to save enough for your console and game. If you add tax, it's 12 weeks — roughly three months, or the length of summer break.

But it's summer and you'll also want to go to a movie every week — $15 — and have a little money to go to the batting cages or meet your friends for a milkshake — another $10. So now, you've got $25 for spending every week and $25 to save for the thing you want. Now, instead of 12 weeks, saving for your console and game is going to take 24 weeks, or six months.

That's a long time. There are a couple of things you can do to make it happen faster. If you add two more lawns and put that money into savings, it will take you less than 12 weeks. If you only go to movies every other week, you're adding another $30 to your savings every month. You could charge more for your mowing and save faster. You could add dog walking to your offerings.

The point is that when you are working and saving toward a goal, you are in control of when you get something. You're not in control if you spend all your time begging your parents to buy it for you. The thing you want is just one of literally dozens of things they are working and saving toward. You may get it, but only after fights and arguments and disappointment. And chances are pretty good that you'll lose interest.

But if you save up for something yourself, you'll appreciate the work and discipline it took to get it. You'll love it even more. You'll take better care of it. It will mean a whole lot more to you, and the experience of saving will put you ahead of a lot of the kids you know. It will put you ahead of most adults when you get into the real world.

Plus, you'll get the things you want by earning them, which feels pretty amazing.

❖

Do Your Homework First

You know that feeling you get on Sunday nights? It's that pit in your stomach panic about going back to school, and it sucks. You've had a good weekend, but now reality is kicking back in, and you don't like it.

Do you know what makes that feeling way worse? Having to do homework.

It might have felt pretty good to put it off for later on Friday and Saturday, but now you want to soak up the last couple hours of your Sunday and, instead, you have to sit down and do work.

I get it. You get home from school on Friday, and you're tired or looking forward to going to a game or hanging out with your friends. You just got through a long week. The last thing you want to do is more homework. Saturday you're busy. You've got sports or work or parties or whatever. Sunday comes, and there's still more you want to do.

But then you're stuck and don't have any options left. You have to do it.

Putting off your homework is bad for a few reasons:

What if something happens on Sunday night — the power goes out, the stores are closed, and you need something for a project, whatever — and you can't get your work done? Now you're up a creek.

It puts you in a bad mood when you should be at your most relaxed.

Getting things done at the last minute stresses you and your parents out. They want to enjoy their Sunday evening too. They don't want to be helping you do homework. They will, of course, but they probably want to watch TV too.

Instead, you can get it done and out of the way. Here are a few things to try to help put an end to the Sunday night homework panic:

Make a plan. As soon as you get home from school on Friday, open up your planner and make a plan for getting your homework done over the course of the weekend. Do a little bit — a third — that night, right away. Do a third on Saturday. Do a third on Sunday morning. Bam. You're done and can finish off your weekend relaxed.

Silence that voice in your head. Procrastination is the result of little deals we make with ourselves. "I'll play now and do my homework later." Or, "I'll do my homework Sunday night because I'll want to do it then." No, you won't, and you know it. When you start bargaining with yourself, you should know it's time to just do the thing you don't want to do.

Be Nike: Just do it. Waiting is always worse. It's always worse doing the thing you don't want to do because, even if you don't realize it, it's in the back of your head. Knowing you have something hard to do and putting it off just adds a level of anger and dread that makes that thing worse than if you had just taken care of it. You are not as tired or busy as you think you are. The work is not as hard as you think it will be. Just do it and move on.

Get in the habit of doing your homework first and then, when you are an adult, you'll have the muscle memory and take care of the hard stuff so that it doesn't spoil the fun stuff.

Return the Text

There are about a thousand ways to get in touch with people these days, and a few years from now, there will be thousands more. You're growing up at a time your grandparents could never have imagined, and your parents are doing their best to understand. Your device gives you access to the sum total of the world's knowledge — good and bad — and all kinds of ways to communicate with your friends, families, coaches, teachers and complete strangers. It's a lot of possibility, a lot of responsibility and a lot to keep up with.

Trying to keep up is hard, but there are a few rules you should always follow:

Never ask for pictures of someone else's body. If you receive them, delete them and tell whoever sent it that it's not cool. If they send pictures of someone else's body, tell an adult. It's not just bad news; it's a crime and has life-ruining potential impacts.

Never tell a stranger who you are, where you live, how old you are or who is at home. There is nothing good that can come of this and only bad things can happen. To that end, never share any of this information online. I know it sounds lame, but you cannot understand how many creepers, peepers and criminals are out there. Don't share anything that might let someone figure out who you are.

Return the text.

This last one is important. If a friend or family member — your mom, dad, brother, sister, grandma or grandpa — takes the time to reach out to you, you have to acknowledge that they did so. If your mom asks if you are okay, tell her you are. Use more than one word. Tell her what you're doing. Don't ignore her. If your grandma wishes you a happy birthday, thank her and tell her what your plans are for the day.

Don't be A ONE-WORD JERK. Don't leave the people who care about you hanging. It might be a drag or a pain but communicating with your loved ones shows them you care. How you communicate with them shows them how much you care.

Use Complete Sentences

Something odd happens when you get into your teenage years: You stop talking. You start communicating in a series of grunts, eye rolls and single syllable replies.

It's annoying and rude to everybody but you.

Making things worse is the tendency to communicate in text — messages, notes, snaps, whatever.

It doesn't matter if you don't mean to be rude. It doesn't matter if you have positivity in your heart. One-word answers, grunts and shorthand come across as you not being interested or engaged.

Use complete sentences.

If someone asks if you had a good day, say, "I did…" and then give some details.

If someone asks if you want to do something, say, "Yes, what time?" or "No, I can't, I'm sorry."

If someone asks you to do something for them, don't say, "Okay." Say, "No problem. I'd be happy to."

Also, never, under any circumstances, text "K" when what you mean is, "Okay." "K" is as lazy as you possibly can be. Don't do it.

You may not feel like having a long discussion. You may be annoyed with the question or the person asking it. Neither is an excuse for being rude.

Conversely, you may be excited or interested in the question, conversation or person. Act like it.

Grunting and being dismissive is not nearly as cool as you think it is.

The Game Is Over When Your Shower Is Done

There's nothing better than winning a game; losing feels like a kick in the stomach. But here's the thing: No matter how big the win or the loss, neither will change your life forever.

Be a good winner. Congratulate the other side. Congratulate your teammates. Don't be the guy who rubs it in. Act like you've won something before. After the game, celebrate with your team and listen to your coach — they will have something to say.

Be a good loser as well. Congratulate the other side. Pat your teammates on the back. Don't be the guy who pouts. Act like you've lost something before. After the game, be a leader on your team and listen to your coach — they will have something to say.

If you're excited because you won or sad because you lost, you're allowed to feel it on the way home. Cherish the excitement and learn from the sadness. When you get home, take off your uniform, jump in the shower and move on. By the time you get dressed, be thinking about what's next — the next game, the next season, homework, dinner, whatever.

Winning and losing are events, not definitions. Don't let them define you. Let how you react to winning and losing show the person and athlete that you are and want to be.

If You See a Problem, Fix It

You don't have to be a hero, but you should act like a citizen.

If you see trash on the floor, don't walk past it. Pick it up and throw it away. If your dog poops in the yard, make a bag glove and pick it up. If you see a faucet left on, check to see if anyone is around and, if not, turn it off.

It doesn't have to be complicated, but if you notice something out of place or something that should be thrown away, take care of it.

Your parents and family will appreciate it.

Your teachers will appreciate it.

Other people will appreciate it.

But more than that, it sets the tone for the man you will become. The habits you make right now will directly affect your potential for success in the future. I know it doesn't seem that way, but it's true. I know you don't want to think about these things, but fixing the little things without being told demonstrates that you take pride in your surroundings, have a good sense of responsibility and accountability and are action-oriented … all things, coaches, colleges, employers and partners will look for in the people they choose to invest in.

So, if there's a candy wrapper on the basement carpet, throw it away. Be a problem solver, not a problem ignorer.

Take Showers

You may not realize it, but you stink.

Your body is producing all kinds of hormones on overtime. You've got hair growing in weird places, you're sweating like it's going out of style and you're spending a lot of time in schools, locker rooms and other places where you're surrounded by other stinky guys.

Trust me, you stink.

You may think that cologne or Axe Body Spray does the trick, but it doesn't. Those things stink too — sometimes worse than your hormone-drenched, sweaty boy smell.

The only answer is hygiene. Take a shower every morning before school. Brush your teeth twice a day. Wash your hair. Scrub your face.

There's nothing more off-putting — to parents, teachers, coaches, girls and other guys — than a boy who stinks, has greasy hair, an oily face and a mop on his head. Take care of yourself. Being clean and not stinking may not make you more popular, successful or loved, but not being clean and stinking to high heaven will hurt your reputation.

Don't be the stinky kid. Don't be the dirtbag. You may think it makes you cool, but you are wrong.

Take a shower. Keep it short. Use soap. Look and smell like a man among boys and, for the love God, no body spray.

You're Not a Jerk

You're not a jerk.

If you've read this book, there's no way you're a jerk. If you've managed to get this far, you must care enough to be worried about being a jerk. And if you care about whether or not you're a jerk, you're not a jerk.

You're not a jerk if you respect yourself. You're not a jerk if you care about other people. You're not a jerk if you explore the world you live in and try to leave things better than you found them. You're not a jerk.

When given a choice between being funny but mean or quiet and kind, keep your mouth shut.

When someone invests themselves in you — romantically, financially or just by having you over — respect them and their investment.

When given a choice between working hard or taking it easy, do the work.

When someone is speaking to you, listen; when they reach out to you, answer them.

When you're playing, play hard, play to win, but know that winning is temporary and being a good sport lasts forever.

When you show up, show up prepared and ready.

When you see something wrong, fix it.

When you see someone hurting, try to help them, but also take care not to let their hurt ruin you.

When you have something to do, do it.

If you do these things more often than not, you won't be a jerk. If you spend your life practicing getting better and better, doing these things most of the time, then almost every time, you won't be a jerk.

Being a jerk is easy, miserable and, ultimately, lonely. Not being a jerk is a little harder, but it is always, always worth it.

Every day, a thousand times a day, you face choices between doing the right thing and the wrong thing. A jerk does the wrong thing. But you don't because you know that doing the right thing is always the right thing to do.

You're not a jerk, so don't be one.

Thank you …

To Jack, Dylan and CJ for trying hard to not be jerks. To Molly Jo, whose book is coming soon. To my dad for not being a jerk and to my wife, Becca, for caring as much as I do about our kids not being jerks.

To Peter Raber for a fantastic cover. You'll be reading his work very soon.

To Katheran Wasson for great editing and even better suggestions.

To KoolAid, John, Hartsock, Janeck, Matty, Jason, Charlie, Whitt, Doug, Moebes and all the other men out there doing their best to raise their boys to be men, not jerks.

Also by Craig J. Heimbuch

For Younger Readers

The Red-Eyed Monster Bass (Kindle & Paperback, 2017)
The Backpack (Kindle & Paperback, 2017)
The Mysterious Cases of Thaddeus & Chuck: B.F.Never
(Kindle & Paperback, 2018)
Random Acts of Mojo (Kindle & Paperback, 2019)
The Mysterious Cases of Thaddeus & Chuck: Jock Itch
(Kindle & Paperback, 2020)

For Young Adults

Fat Boy's Last Meal (Kindle & Paperback, 2017)

For Adults

Chasing Oliver Hazard Perry: Travels in the Footsteps of
the Lucky Commodore who Saved America (Clerisy, 2010)
And Now We Shall Do Manly Things (Wm. Morrow/Harper
Collins, 2012)
Some People Should Eat Their Young (Kindle, 2013)
Above All Things, Be Useful (Kindle, 2014)
Pitch Please: Tell Stories that Stick (Kindle & Paperback 2019)
Being a Ghost: Advice and Adventures for People who
Write for Other People (Kindle & Paperback 2020)

About Craig J. Heimbuch

Craig J. Heimbuch is an award-winning author and journalist, best-selling ghostwriter, husband of one and father of four. He writes stories about adventure and travel, whether through his adult non-fiction or fiction stories for younger readers, and he knows no greater joy than setting out for parts unknown with a thirst for discovery and a passion for new experiences.

He is the recipient of the Best Non-Fiction Award from the Great Lakes Booksellers Association for his first book, "Chasing Oliver Hazard Perry" as well as several awards for his in-depth and feature writing from his time as a newspaper and magazine writer. He's been described as "exactly what American travel writing needs" by former Esquire editor Will Blythe, and Publisher's Weekly described his writing as "sometimes funny, sometimes bittersweet, and always well-paced adventures."

This is the 17th book he's written and his first non-fiction book for young readers.

Send him an email at letterstocraig@gmail.com. He'd love to hear from you on Instagram (@cheimbuch) too.

Made in the USA
Middletown, DE
27 September 2021